Studies in 2 Peter

By Michael Penny

ISBN: 978-1-78364-519-0

www.obt.org.uk

****

THE OPEN BIBLE TRUST
Fordland Mount, Upper Basildon,
Reading, RG8 8LU, UK.

Studies in 2 Peter

Contents

Introduction

Introduction

To whom did Peter write?

In 2 Peter 3:1 we read that this was the second letter that he wrote to these people, and we know that the first letter was written, "To God's elect, strangers in the world, *scattered* throughout Pontus, Galatia, Cappadocia, Asia and Bithynia," (1 Peter 1:1). The word 'scattered' is the Greek *diaspora* and is a technical term referring to those Jews who were scattered throughout the Roman Empire and beyond. James also addressed his letter to them, and his opening makes it clear that he is also writing to the people of Israel. His opening verses states, "To the twelve tribes *scattered* among the nations" (James 1:1). However, it is a great shame that some translations mask this important piece of information. For example, the opening of James in the *Good News Bible* is, "to all God's people scattered over the whole world". However, its opening of Peter's first letter is better: "To God's chosen people who live as refugees through the provinces of ..."

When it comes to 'interpreting' a particular part of the Bible, we are more likely to have a better understanding of it if we are aware of the people to whom it was written and the ministry of the writer. From the Bible we see that Peter had little to do with Gentiles. Although he went to the first Gentile, the God fearing Cornelius (Acts 10), he and the rest of the church in Jerusalem seemed somewhat concerned when other Gentiles were evangelised in Antioch. They sent Barnabas to investigate and when some time later Peter went to Antioch, he withdrew from meeting with the Gentile Christians (Galatians 2:11-13).

It is Paul who was given a special ministry to the Gentiles and is the only person called 'the apostle to the Gentiles' (Romans 11:13; Galatians 2:8). In fact we have a clear agreement between Paul and Barnabas, on the one hand, and Peter, James and John, on the other. Galatians was probably written from Antioch, after Paul returned from his first missionary journey[1] (Acts 14:26-28). In that letter he refers to a meeting he and Barnabas had had with those three which had taken place before he had embarked on that journey.

> On the contrary, they saw that I had been entrusted with the task of preaching the gospel to the Gentiles, just as Peter had been to the Jews. For God, who was at work in the ministry of Peter as an apostle to the Jews, was also at work in my ministry as an apostle to the Gentiles. James, Peter and John, those reputed to be pillars, gave me and Barnabas the right hand of fellowship when they recognized the grace given to me. They agreed that we should go to the Gentiles, and they to the Jews. (Galatians 2:7-9)

Not only was this agreed amongst themselves, it was also sanctioned by the Holy Spirit. On returning to Antioch, the Spirit told them to "Set apart for me Barnabas and Saul for the work to which I have called them" (Acts 13:2). Paul, then, was to go to the Gentile nations and minister to those there – both Jews and Gentiles in accord with his commission (Acts 9:15; see also 26:20). Peter, James and John, then, ministered to the people of

---

[1] As one of the main issues in Galatians deals with the fact that Gentile Christians did not have to be circumcised, it is hard to see how Galatians could have been written *after* the Jerusalem Council of Acts 15. If it had been, Paul could have referred to it, to support his argument.

Israel, and their writings, and those of Jude, are specifically addressed to the people of Israel. In fact the word 'Gentile' is not used in the letters of James, Peter, John and Jude.

This means that we, as Gentiles, may find parts of their writings more difficult to understand and some parts may not apply to us. They are certainly more difficult to understand than Paul's letters, although they have much in common with his earlier ones; i.e. Romans, 1 & 2 Corinthians, Galatians and 1 & 2 Thessalonians. These were sent to churches which had a mixture of Jewish and Gentile Christians. Paul's later letters, on the other hand, are probably the easiest to understand. These seven – Ephesians, Philippians, Colossians, 1 & 2 Timothy, Titus and Philemon – were written at or after the end of Acts when distinctions between Jews and Gentiles were abolished.

When did Peter write?

Both of Peter's letters were written to Jewish Christians during the time covered by the Acts of the Apostles. They were written at the time when they still hoped that Christ would return during their life time. Letters written during the Acts period refer to Christ's second coming and many mention its nearness, and the problems and difficulties which will precede it. For example, consider the following quotations:

> Romans 13:11-12: And do this, understanding the present time. The hour has come for you to wake up from your slumber, because our salvation is nearer now than when we first believed. *The night is nearly over; the day is almost here.* So let us put aside the deeds of darkness and put on the armour of light.

1 Corinthians 7:26-31. Because of the present crisis, I think that it is good for you to remain as you are. Are you married? Do not seek a divorce. Are you unmarried? Do not look for a wife. But if you do marry, you have not sinned; and if a virgin marries, she has not sinned. But those who marry will face many troubles in this life, and I want to spare you this. What I mean, brothers, is that *the time is short*. From now on those who have wives should live as if they had none; those who mourn, as if they did not; those who are happy, as if they were not; those who buy something, as if it were not theirs to keep; those who use the things of the world, as if not engrossed in them. For this *world in its present form is passing away*.

1 Corinthians 10:11: These things happened to them as examples and were written down as warnings for us, on whom *the fulfilment of the ages has come*.

Hebrews 10:36-38: You need to persevere so that when you have done the will of God, you will receive what he has promised. For in just a very little while, *"He who is coming will come and will not delay. But my righteous one will live by faith. And if he shrinks back, I will not be pleased with him."*

James 5:8-9: You too, be patient and stand firm, because *the Lord's coming is near*. Don't grumble against each other, brothers, or you will be judged. *The Judge is standing at the door*!

1 Peter 4:7: *The end of all things is near*. Therefore be clear minded and self-controlled so that you can pray.

1 John 2:18: Dear children, *this is the last hour*; and as you have heard that the antichrist is coming, even now many antichrists have come. This is how we know *it is the last hour*.

Revelation 1:1-3: The revelation of Jesus Christ, which God gave him to show his servants what *must soon take place*. He made it known by sending his angel to his servant John, who testifies to everything he saw - that is, the word of God and the testimony of Jesus Christ. Blessed is the one who reads the words of this prophecy, and blessed are those who hear it and take to heart what is written in it, because *the time is near*.

Revelation 22:10: Then he told me, "Do not seal up the words of the prophecy of this book, because *the time is near*." (Contrast with Daniel 8:26 and 12:4)

However, such expressions as those indicated above in italics, stating that the last days are near, are absent from Paul's seven letters written at the end or after Acts. Paul does, however, refer to both the 'latter times' and 'last days' in 1 Timothy 4:1 and 2 Timothy 3:1, but in neither does he say that they are near. Why is that? What changed? The answer to that question lies in Peter's speech at the start of Acts. Addressing the "Men of Israel" (Acts 3:12), Peter exhorted them to:

"Repent, then, and turn to God, so that your sins may be wiped out, that times of refreshing may come from the Lord, and that he may send the Christ, who has been appointed for you - even Jesus. He must remain in heaven until the time comes for God to restore everything, as he promised long ago through his holy prophets." (Acts 3:19-21)

Here Peter exhorted them to repent, principally of their sin of rejecting Jesus as the Christ (Messiah) and Son of God. If they did so, not only would their sins be wiped out but God would send Christ Jesus back to them. Thus we see great energy expounded throughout the Acts period on evangelism to Jews, both in the land and also those dispersed abroad – the ones to whom Peter wrote. So what had happened?

Although many Jews did repent and believe in Jesus, many did not, especially those of the leadership. First of all God sent people like Peter and Paul to a few Gentiles, and the purpose of this was to provoke the Jews into faith (Romans 11:11-14). The Jewish leaders rejected Christ when He was on earth and hardened their hearts to His ministry and miracles. Similarly, the Jewish leadership of the Acts period, both those in the land and those in the synagogues scattered throughout the world, continued to reject the ministry and miracles of the Apostles. So much so that, at the end of Acts, we have the last New Testament pronouncement of the judgmental prophecy from Isaiah 6. There Luke wrote:

> They [the leaders of the Jews in Rome] arranged to meet Paul on a certain day, and came in even larger numbers to the place where he was staying. From morning till evening he explained and declared to them the kingdom of God and tried to convince them about Jesus from the Law of Moses and from the Prophets. Some were convinced by what he said, but others would not believe. They disagreed among themselves and began to leave after Paul had made this final statement: "The Holy Spirit spoke the truth to

your forefathers when he said through Isaiah the prophet: `Go to this people and say, "You will be ever hearing but never understanding; you will be ever seeing but never perceiving." For this people's heart has become calloused; they hardly hear with their ears, and they have closed their eyes. Otherwise they might see with their eyes, hear with their ears, understand with their hearts and turn, and I would heal them.' Therefore I want you to know that God's salvation has been sent to the Gentiles, and they will listen!" (Acts 28:23-28)

These Jews had so hardened their hearts that they were blind to the significance of the miracles[2] and deaf to the arguments from Scripture. From that point on God turned to the Gentiles and we read next that Paul spent another two years under house arrest (Acts 28:30). During those two years he wrote Ephesians, Colossians, Philemon and Philippians and, a little later, wrote 1 & 2 Timothy and Titus.

Peter wrote to the scattered Jews *before* this momentous event.

Why did Peter write?

He states the reason for writing in the opening words of Chapter 3.

> Dear friends, this is now my second letter to you. I have written both of them as reminders to stimulate you to wholesome thinking. I want you to recall the words spoken in the past by the holy prophets and the command

---

[2] For more on the significance of the miraculous signs of the New Testament see *The Miracles of the Apostles* by Michael Penny (OBT).

given by our Lord and Saviour through your apostles. (2 Peter 3:1-2)

As stated earlier, there may be some parts of this letter that we will have difficulty understanding, and there may be some parts which will not apply to us. However, as Peter's main purpose was to "stimulate ... wholesome thinking", there will undoubtedly be things we can learn and apply to our lives. Whether we recall the words of the prophets may well depend upon how well we know what the prophets wrote, and I wonder to which command of Christ Peter was referring to?

2 Peter

Chapter 1

2 Peter Chapter 1

2 Peter 1:1: **Simon Peter, a servant and apostle of Jesus Christ, To those who through the righteousness of our God and Saviour Jesus Christ have received a faith as precious as ours:**

Peter introduces himself as a 'servant' of Jesus Christ and as an 'apostle' of Jesus Christ. The word for 'servant' is *doulos* which means "a slave; literal or figurative, involuntary or voluntary; frequently, therefore in a qualified sense of subjection or subservience" (Strong).

Peter may have considered himself a slave of Jesus Christ as Christ had redeemed him from the power of sin, death and Satan (1 Peter 1:18-19). At that time, some people redeemed slaves. They could go to a slave market, purchase a slave and let him or her go free. Christ had redeemed Peter and set him free, but Peter, like some of those redeemed slaves, voluntarily put himself into the service of the One who had redeemed him and set him free. And that One had commissioned Peter as an Apostle to the Jews.

> On the contrary, they saw that I [Paul] had been entrusted with the task of preaching the gospel to the Gentiles, just as Peter had been to the Jews. For God, who was at work in the ministry of Peter as an apostle to the Jews, was also at work in my ministry as an apostle to the Gentiles. (Galatians 2:7-8)

So Peter's commission was to preach the gospel to the Jews and be an apostle to the Jews. And Peter addressed those Jewish Christians as "those who through the righteousness of our God and Saviour Jesus Christ have received a faith as precious as ours". Here Peter, although a Christ appointed Apostle to these people, does not elevate himself above them when it comes to their common faith or the righteousness of God. Both the *KJV* and the *ASV* make this clearer by stating that they have "obtained like precious faith with us". And the *NASV* makes it even clearer; "those who have received a faith of the same kind as ours".

> To those who have obtained a faith of equal in standing with ours. (*ESV*)

It makes no difference who a person is, whatever their position in life. Their faith is of equal standing, and so is "the righteousness that comes from God and is by faith" (Philippians 3:9).

2 Peter 1:2: Grace and peace be yours in abundance through the knowledge of God and of Jesus our Lord.

Peace (Hebrew *shalom*; Greek *eirene*) was the common Hebrew greeting. When we use the word we usually define it in a negative sense; the absence of war or hostility or terrorism. However, to the Jews it was a very positive peace; it was an inner peace; the peace that comes from godliness and contentment; the peace that came from God and which passed all understanding (Philippians 4:7).

To this 'peace', Peter added 'grace', and some of his readers may have struggled with this. For years they had been taught that righteousness came from obedience to the Law and had to be earned. However, that was wrong teaching and, like the Apostle Paul, even though he was considered righteous by many because of his obedience to the Law, he learnt that legalistic righteousness was as "rubbish" (*NIV*) or "dung" (*KJV*) compared to the righteousness of God which is by grace through faith (Philippians 3:4-9).

> This righteousness from God comes through faith in Jesus Christ to **all** who believe. There is no difference, for all have sinned and fall short of the glory of God. (Romans 3:22-23)

Just as Peter, the Apostle to the Jews, saw that those to whom he wrote had a faith equal to his, so Paul, the Apostle to the Gentiles, saw that there was no difference in the righteousness God gave to all who had faith in Christ Jesus.

However, as mentioned above, some of Peter's readers, being Jewish, may have struggled with this. They needed to be taught and given understanding. They had faith but it was "through knowledge" of God and knowing what Christ achieved on the Cross that they would have peace of mind, and would ensure that they appreciated peace and grace in abundance. Even today, some Christians are not fully convinced that all their sins have been forgiven because of the all sufficiency of Christ's sacrifice for sin. We should not condemn or criticise such believers. We should gently teach them, giving them a greater knowledge and a deeper understanding of God's character and Christ's work so that they can enjoy the consequences of grace and the peace of God in abundance.

2 Peter 1:3: **His divine power has given us everything we need for life and godliness through our knowledge of him who called us by his own glory and goodness.**

To what divine 'power' is Peter referring? Paul prayed that the Ephesians may know "his incomparably great power for us who believe" and went on to say "that power is like the working of his mighty strength, which he exerted in Christ when he raised him from the dead and seated him at his right hand in the heavenly realms" (Ephesians 1:19-20). And later we read:

> I pray that out of his glorious riches he may strengthen you with power through his Spirit in your inner being. (Ephesians 3:16)

Thus this power is available to all believers in Christ. In Philippians 4:19 we read that "God will meet all your *needs* according to his glorious riches in Christ Jesus". Thus both Peter and Paul see God, either through the Holy Spirit or through Christ, meeting all the needs of His people.
Christ, through His work, conquered sin and death, and so met the need for forgiveness and eternal life.

The indwelling Holy Spirit strengthens believers with power in their inner being so that "Christ may dwell in their hearts through faith" and gives them power to "grasp how wide and long and high and deep is the love of Christ and to know (or acknowledge) this love which passes understanding" (Ephesians 3:16-19). To put that love into practice, to acknowledge it, that is godliness, and people cannot do it in their own strength. Thus Paul wrote, telling them, "To be filled with the Spirit" (Ephesians 5:18). They had the Spirit, (Ephesians 1:13-14), but did they let the Spirit fill them?

Here, in verse 3, Peter again refers to our "knowledge" of God, and this was so important for these early Jewish Christians. We must remember that they did not have a complete New Testament. By the time Peter wrote this second letter they may have had a gospel or two; they probably had had the letter from

James and maybe one or two others, including some from Paul, probably Galatians (2 Peter 3:15-16; and note 'Galatia' in 1 Peter 1:1). However, they had centuries of traditions to rethink and they had to unlearn the teaching of the Pharisees. Thus their 'knowledge' of what God was like had to be re-learnt.

These Jewish sinners were given divine power by the "glory and goodness" of God. Did they appreciate that? Could they grasp it? Did they believe it?

People, both Jews and Gentiles of the first century, and even some Christians today, simply cannot accept just how much God loves them and forgives them. In Ephesians Paul wrote about God's 'glorious' grace, the 'riches' of God's grace which he 'lavished' on us, about God's 'great' love for us, and God being 'rich' in mercy (Ephesians 1:6-7; 2:4). These are the things we need to know, understand and believe, and those Jewish Christians to whom Peter wrote needed the full assurance of their security in Christ.

2 Peter 1:4: **Through these he has given us his very great and precious promises, so that through them you may participate in the divine nature and escape the corruption in the world caused by evil desires.**

Peter does not spell out the "very great and precious promises" he is referring to. Some promises made to Israel in the Old Testament certainly do not apply to Gentile Christians today. Even some of the promises in the New Testament did not apply to Gentile Christians of that time, let alone to Christians today. As examples we shall consider three such promises.

Promise 1: Matthew 6:31-33:

> "So do not worry, saying, 'What shall we eat?' or 'What shall we drink?' or 'What shall we wear?' For the pagans run after all these things, and your heavenly Father knows that you need them. But seek first his kingdom and his righteousness, and all these things will be given to you as well."

The "all these things" promised to those who seek first God's kingdom and righteousness are, from the context, clearly limited to food, drink and clothing. I have never gone without food, drink and clothing – even when I was not a Christian. Many in the secular, industrialised society are not believers and yet they are well fed and well clothed. However, many believers in other parts of the world are under-fed, suffer from malnutrition and some have died of starvation.

The words of Matthew 6:31-33 are based upon a promise given to Israel in Deuteronomy 28. If they fully obeyed they would be blessed with such things as good crops and healthy animals. However, if they did not, their crops would fail and they would go without such things. The leaders of Israel rejected Christ and put Him on the Cross. During the Acts period they imprisoned and beat people like Peter and John and Paul and stoned Stephen and beheaded James. Thus it is no surprise that we read of a great famine which seriously afflicted Israel (Acts 11:28).

Promise 2: Luke 21:12-15:

> "But before all this, they will lay hands on you and persecute you. They will deliver you to synagogues and prisons, and you will be brought before kings and

governors, and all on account of my name. This will result in your being witnesses to them. But make up your mind not to worry beforehand how you will defend yourselves. For I will give you words and wisdom that none of your adversaries will be able to resist or contradict."

This promise was given primarily to the Apostles, but other Jews clearly benefitted from it. Peter and John defended themselves so well against the accusations of the rulers, elders, teachers of the law and the high priest and his family that we read:

When they saw the courage of Peter and John and realized that they were unschooled, ordinary men, they were astonished and they took note that these men had been with Jesus. (Acts 4:13)

And we can see this in Stephen's speech before the Sanhedrin (Acts 7) and Paul, within days of his conversion, "grew more and more powerful and baffled the Jews living in Damascus by proving that Jesus is the Christ" (Acts 9:22). We read of no Gentiles making such speeches and arguing so forcefully or convincingly and we today know that we have to study and prepare for any public sermon or study, speech or lecture, we may give.

Promise 3: John 14:12-14

"I tell you the truth, anyone who has faith in me will do what I have been doing. He will do even greater things than these, because I am going to the Father. And I will do whatever you ask in my name, so that the Son may bring glory to the Father. You may ask me for anything in my name, and I will do it."

The Lord told the Twelve that "at the renewal of all things, when the Son of Man sits on his glorious throne, you who have followed me will also sit on twelve thrones, judging the twelve tribes of Israel" (Matthew 19:28). Christians today do not apply that promise to themselves, because it was clearly given to the Twelve, but so, too, was the one in John 14:12-14. We do not do greater things than Christ; we do not get whatever we ask in His name. Yet if we read through the Acts of the Apostles we do see the Apostles healing the sick and raising the dead. We see them imparting the Holy Spirit, which may be what Christ was referring to when He said they would do greater things than He did. We also see some spectacular answers to prayer.

Thus we must be careful with the words of 2 Peter 1:4. However, there may be other promises that Peter could be alluding to which are relevant; for example, the promised Holy Spirit. Not only were the Jews and Gentiles of the Acts Period promised the Holy Spirit (Acts 1:4-5; Galatians 3:14), but believers today are sealed with the Spirit when they believe the gospel of salvation (Ephesians 1:13-14). However, the working of the Holy Spirit today may well be different from that of the Acts Period.[3]

> "Therefore come out from them and be separate", says the Lord. "Touch no unclean thing, and I will receive you. *I will be a Father* to you, and you will be my sons and daughters, says the Lord Almighty." Since we have these promises, dear friends, let us purify ourselves from everything that contaminates body and spirit, perfecting holiness out of reverence for God. (2 Corinthians 6:17-18 & 7:1)

---

[3] See *The Work of the Holy Spirit in an Age of Grace* by Michael Penny and published by The Open Bible Trust.

This promise of God's fatherhood, quoted from 2 Samuel 7:8,14, was true not only of David in the Old Testament and the people to whom Paul was writing. It is also true of the people to whom Peter was writing and is true for us today. It is this type of promise that Peter probably had in mind for he wanted them to appreciate such a promise and "escape the corruption in the world caused by evil desires", similar to sentiments expressed by Paul in 2 Corinthians.

Paul also wrote about "the *promise* of life that is in Christ Jesus" (2 Timothy 1:1) and John wrote "this is what he *promised* us - even eternal life" (1 John 2:25). At the start of his letter to Titus, Paul wrote about a "the knowledge of the truth that leads to godliness - a faith and knowledge resting on the hope of eternal life, which God, who does not lie, *promised* before the beginning of time" (Titus 1:1-2).

James also wrote of a promise:

> "Blessed is the man who perseveres under trial, because when he has stood the test, he will receive the crown of life that God has *promised* to those who love him" (James 1:12).

All such promises as these are true for all time and for all who believe in Christ. They should inspire us to godliness and to turn our backs on sin and put away evil desires. Then we will escape the corruption of this world, which was what Peter wanted for his readers.

2 Peter 1:5-8: **For this very reason, make every effort to**

> **add to your faith goodness;**
> > **and to goodness, knowledge;**
> **and to knowledge, self-control;**
> > **and to self-control, perseverance;**
> **and to perseverance, godliness;**
> > **and to godliness, brotherly kindness;**
> > > **and to brotherly kindness, love.**

For if you possess these qualities in increasing measure, they will keep you from being ineffective and unproductive in your knowledge of our Lord Jesus Christ.

The teaching in these verses needs little comment. They set out a pathway that is universal for all Christians, Jews and Gentiles, for all time, for the Acts Period and for today. The goal is 'love', true *agape* love; the love of 1 Corinthians 13; the self-sacrificing love of Christ as set forth in Philippians 2:5-8.

However, note that we have yet another reference to 'knowledge'. Paul also links 'love' and 'knowledge' in his prayer for the Philippians.

> And this is my prayer: that your love may abound more and more in knowledge and depth of insight, so that you may be able to discern what is best and may be pure and blameless until the day of Christ, filled with the fruit of righteousness that comes through Jesus Christ - to the glory and praise of God. (Philippians 1:9-11)

It was necessary for those early Jewish and Gentile Christians to be taught, to acquire knowledge about the character of God and, especially for the pagan Gentiles who had come to believe, to know what constituted goodness and godliness, and why kindness should develop into love.

It was also important for them to persevere. These early Jewish Christians were experiencing persecution, not from the Romans (Roman persecution did not start until after AD 60) but from the Sanhedrin and synagogue rulers. Christ prophesied that this would be the case (Luke 21: 12); James also wrote about it, and the letter to the Hebrews deals with it; e.g. Hebrews 10:33-34; James 1:3,12; 2:6-7; 5:4-6.

Paul also wrote to the believers in Romans about suffering and perseverance. They, within a few short years of receiving the letter, were to suffer terribly at the hands of Nero. We read:

> Not only so, but we also rejoice in our sufferings, because we know that
>> suffering produces perseverance;
>>> perseverance, character;
>>>> and character, hope.
> And hope does not disappoint us, because God has poured out his love into our hearts by the Holy Spirit, whom he has given us. (Romans 5:3-5)

However, Peter's point was that they needed to possess these qualities in increasing measure. The *NASV* translates verse 8 as follows:

> For if these qualities are yours and are increasing, they render you neither useless nor unfruitful in the true knowledge of our Lord Jesus Christ.

Thus such qualities as goodness, self-control, perseverance, godliness, kindness and love are what Christians need if they are not to be useless in their witness, nor unfruitful in the knowledge of Christ Jesus.

Knowledge is important and Paul warned of those that "are zealous for God, but their zeal is *not* based on knowledge" (Romans 10:2). Thus it seems believers can be zealous for unimportant things and so their knowledge of God, which can be gleaned only from the Bible, is not only important, it is also essential.

However, Paul also wrote that "Knowledge puffs up, but love builds up" (1 Corinthians 8:1). We have already seen, in such places as 2 Peter 1:5-7 and Philippians 1:9 that knowledge should lead to a greater appreciation of love and an acknowledgement, i.e. a putting into practice, of that love (Ephesians 3:17-19). Thus if our study of the Bible, if our greater understanding of the plan and purpose of God, does not lead to a greater love for God, our wives or husbands, our fellow Christians, our neighbours and our enemies ... what is its value?

2 Peter 1:9: **But if anyone does not have them, he is near-sighted and blind, and has forgotten that he has been cleansed from his past sins.**

However, it seems that some in Peter's day, and probably some today, do not have the knowledge of God and did not display such qualities as goodness, self-control, perseverance, godliness, brotherly kindness and love. If that is the case, states Peter, they are near-sighted and blind. They see no further than their nose and the mirror. They have forgotten the great love that God had in giving His only Son so that whoever believes in Him should not perish, but have everlasting life (John 3:16). If God had such great love for us, and if Christ was so willing to give up His home in heaven and to come to earth, to take on human likeness and suffer death on a cross ... our attitude should be the same as His (Philippians 2:5-8).

2 Peter 1:10-11: **Therefore, my brothers, be all the more eager to make your calling and election sure. For if you do these things, you will never fall, and you will receive a rich welcome into the eternal kingdom of our Lord and Saviour Jesus Christ.**

We need to be careful with this translation of verse 10. It could be read as though a person's calling and election, and thus their salvation, was not sure; that he, himself, had to do something to make it sure. However, the *NASV* has the following:

> Therefore, brethren, be all the more diligent to make certain about His calling and choosing you; for as long as you practice these things, you will never stumble.

Thus these people must not forget that Christ has cleansed them from their sins (2 Peter 1:9). They needed to know just how much He loves them and that they are safe and secure in His arms once they have believed in Him. They needed to be diligent, be all the more eager (*NIV*), to make these things certain in their understanding. They should not doubt. They needed to know these things, understand them and be certain of them, and they should possess those qualities mentioned. If they do so, not only will they not be ineffective and unproductive, they will not stumble. Then they will receive a rich welcome and reward.

2 Peter 1:12-15: **So I will always remind you of these things, even though you know them and are firmly established in the truth you now have. I think it is right to refresh your memory as long as I live in the tent of this body, because I know that I will soon put it aside, as our Lord Jesus Christ has made clear to me. And I will make every effort to see that after my departure you will always be able to remember these things.**

Peter was clearly concerned for the Christian Jews of the dispersion. Even though he was convinced that they knew what he had just written and that they were firmly established in the truth, he wanted to remind them, to refresh their memory. They could so easily forget. They did not have the Bible as we have. We can read them and re-read them and, even then, we can forget. There may have been scrolls of the Old Testament in their synagogues, but they were unlikely to possess any personally. Although a number of the New Testament documents would have been written at this time, they would have possessed few of them. Thus it was easy for them to forget.

But the next words would have sent a shiver down their spines. Peter wrote of his impending death. It seems Christ had revealed to him that he was soon to die. However, Peter's concern was for these people. He was to make every effort that even after his death they would be able to remember what he taught them. To some extent he was already doing this by writing to them a letter, and his two letters to them not only outlived him, they also outlived the people he wrote to.

What else may Peter have done? We have no idea about this but just as Paul sent Titus first to Crete and then to Dalmatia, Crescens to Galatia and Tychicus to Ephesus (Titus 1:5; 2 Timothy 4:9-12) so Peter may have sent people, or asked people to write (e.g. the letter to the Hebrews), to these scattered Jews. He may even have asked Paul to do so. Later Paul did write to the Ephesians and Colossians, cities which were in the region of Asia, one of the regions Peter sent his letters to.

2 Peter 1:16-19: **We did not follow cleverly invented stories when we told you about the power and coming of our Lord Jesus Christ, but we were eyewitnesses of his majesty. For he received honour and glory from God the Father when the voice came to him from the Majestic Glory, saying, "This is my Son, whom I love; with him I am well pleased." We ourselves heard this voice that came from heaven when we were with him on the sacred mountain. And we have the word of the prophets made more certain, and you will do well to pay attention to it, as to a light shining in a dark place, until the day dawns and the morning star rises in your hearts.**

Here Peter refers to the second coming of Christ. He refers to it again, later, in 2 Peter 3:3,9-10. It seems some were questioning this teaching. As we mentioned earlier, the teaching at that time was that Christ would return soon. However, by the time Peter wrote this second letter some twenty or so years had gone by and Christ had not returned.

Peter wrote that he had not followed an invented story. In fact he was very sure of what he taught because he had been an eyewitness to Christ's majesty. Here he is referring to Christ's Transfiguration; a vision he, James and John had seen and which is recorded in Matthew 17:1-6 and Mark 9:1-7. The result of seeing this vision and hearing God's voice was that they were more certain about what the prophets had written.

He then goes on to tell his readers that they would do well to pay attention to what they had been told about Christ's Transfiguration and what the prophets had to say. They should pay attention to it until Christ returns; i.e. until the day dawns and the morning star arises in their hearts.

2 Peter 1:20-21: **Above all, you must understand that no prophecy of Scripture came about by the prophet's own interpretation. For prophecy never had its origin in the will of man, but men spoke from God as they were carried along by the Holy Spirit.**

Some may have been doubting what the Old Testament prophets said, but it is more likely that they were questioning those who, at that time, had the gift of prophecy (Romans 12:6; 1 Corinthians 12:10,28 and note Agabus in Acts 11:28; 21:10-11). They may have been saying, as Peter did in Acts 3:19-20 and as Paul and others wrote, that the end was near, the time was short, Christ was to return soon. But Peter had to remind them that such prophecies, those in the Old Testament as well as those in the New Testament Scriptures, were not made up by man. Rather they came from the Holy Spirit (1 Corinthians 12:8-11).

2 Peter
Chapter 2

2 Peter Chapter 2

2 Peter 2:1: **But there were also false prophets among the people, just as there will be false teachers among you. They will secretly introduce destructive heresies, even denying the sovereign Lord who bought them - bringing swift destruction on themselves.**

Here Peter reminds his readers that there were false prophets in Old Testament times, especially in Jeremiah's day. Jeremiah prophesied that the Babylonian's would come and besiege and conquer Jerusalem; the false prophets said they would not. Jeremiah said if they surrendered to the Babylonians, their life would be spared; the false prophets told them not to surrender, but to stay in Jerusalem. See, for example, Jeremiah 14:11-15; 21:9-10; 23:16-17; 23:31-34.

Peter told them there would be false teachers among them. Here he is echoing the words of Christ from Matthew 7:15, where he warned of false prophets coming in sheep's clothing, as did Paul in Acts 20:29. Christ also speaks of false prophets in Matthew 24:11,24 and Acts 13:6 records a false prophet on the island of Cyprus who opposed Paul.

John, in his letter, wrote and warned of one of the earliest heresies concerning the person of Jesus.

> Who is the liar? It is the man who denies that Jesus is the Christ. Such a man is the antichrist - he denies the Father and the Son. No one who denies the Son has the Father; whoever acknowledges the Son has the Father also. (1 John 2:22-23)

Many deceivers, who do not acknowledge Jesus Christ as coming in the flesh, have gone out into the world. Any such person is the deceiver and the antichrist. (2 John 1:7)

Thus to deny Jesus was the Christ (Messiah) was one such false teaching and the other was to deny Christ came in the flesh, that He was truly human. This was the teaching of the Gnostics and as such meant that Christ could not have made the perfect sacrifice for sin and could not have taken on death and conquered it by resurrection. These false prophets and false teachers brought swift destruction upon themselves. Some like Elymas were struck blind (Acts 13:8-11) and John wrote about sins, some of which lead to death (1 John 5:16-17). Here he is not referring to the natural law of 'as you sow, so shall you reap'. Excessive promiscuity and alcohol consumption may well bring illness and early death. Here it is the 'swift' death of judgment, as we see with Ananias and Sapphira, and also with Herod (Acts 5:1-11; 12:19-23). During the Acts period, as well as there being miracles of blessing, there were also miracles of judgment. This is what these false teachers were in danger of.

2 Peter 2:2-3: **Many will follow their shameful ways and will bring the way of truth into disrepute. In their greed these teachers will exploit you with stories they have made up. Their condemnation has long been hanging over them, and their destruction has not been sleeping**.

Sadly Peter stated that many will follow the shameful ways of these false teachers and bring the truth into disrepute. It would seem then that there was false teaching not only about the person of Christ, but in other areas also.

Some of the Christians in Rome were teaching, or were being taught, that as God is gracious and forgiving the more they sinned the greater was God's grace and this exalted God! (See Romans 6:1,15.)

Then in 1 Corinthians 5:1-2: we read:

It is actually reported that there is sexual immorality among you, and of a kind that does not occur even among pagans: A man has his father's wife. And you are proud! Shouldn't you rather have been filled with grief and have put out of your fellowship the man who did this?

Here is a clear example of teaching and behaviour which would bring the way of the truth into disrepute. The Corinthian Christians not only tolerated such sin, but were proud of it!

It would seem that 'greed' was a motive for some of these false teachers. Paul warned of such false teachers who taught what people wanted to hear and, as a result, probably received more money in gifts.

For the time will come when men will not put up with sound doctrine. Instead, to suit their own desires, they will gather around them a great number of teachers to say what their itching ears want to hear. They will turn their ears away from the truth and turn aside to myths. (2 Timothy 4:3-4)

And Paul was also plagued by the false teaching that Gentiles had to be circumcised to be saved, and this was many years after the Jerusalem Council of Acts 15 decreed they did not.

For there are many rebellious people, mere talkers and deceivers, especially those of the circumcision group. They must be silenced, because they are ruining whole households by teaching things they ought not to teach-- and that for the sake of dishonest gain. (Titus 1:10-11)

All such people, during the Acts period, were in danger of condemnation and destruction, i.e. the miraculous judgments of that age. To assure his readers that God was aware of these people and that their judgment was certain, Peter lists a number of incidents from Genesis.

2 Peter 2:4-9: **For if God did not spare angels when they sinned, but sent them to hell, putting them into gloomy dungeons to be held for judgment; if he did not spare the ancient world when he brought the flood on its ungodly people, but protected Noah, a preacher of righteousness, and seven others; if he condemned the cities of Sodom and Gomorrah by burning them to ashes, and made them an example of what is going to happen to the ungodly; and if he rescued Lot, a righteous man, who was distressed by the filthy lives of lawless men (for that righteous man, living among them day after day, was tormented in his righteous soul by the lawless deeds he saw and heard) - if this is so, then the Lord knows how to rescue godly men from trials and to hold the unrighteous for the day of judgment, while continuing their punishment.**

The second and third of these judgments are clear and straightforward - the flood in Noah's day and the destruction of Sodom and Gomorrah – but to what is the first referring? As the second two are from Genesis, it seems sensible that the first also comes from that book, and if they are in chronological order, the first must predate the flood. Peter also wrote of these in his first letter and does link them to the days of Noah.

> For Christ died for sins once for all, the righteous for the unrighteous, to bring you to God. He was put to death in the body but made alive by the Spirit, through whom also he went and preached to the spirits in prison who disobeyed long ago when God waited patiently in the days of Noah while the ark was being built. (1 Peter 3:18-20)

And Jude also refers to them in verse 6.

> And the angels who did not keep their positions of authority but abandoned their own home - these he has kept in darkness, bound with everlasting chains for judgment on the great Day.

So who are these spirits in prison[4]? If the answer lies in Genesis during the days of Noah, then it seems Peter is referring to Genesis 6:1-4.

> When men began to increase in number on the earth and daughters were born to them, *the sons of God* saw that the daughters of men were beautiful, and they married any of them they chose. Then the LORD said, "My Spirit will not contend with man forever, for he is mortal; his days will be a hundred and twenty years." The Nephilim were on the earth in those days - and also afterwards - when *the sons of God* went to the daughters of men and had children by them. They were the heroes of old, men of renown.

---

[4] For a full treatment of this subject see *The Spirits in Prison* by E W Bullinger published by The Open Bible Trust.

The expression 'the sons of God' may refer to the 'angels that sinned', 'the angels who ... abandoned their home' in heaven, 'the spirits in prison'.

Peter wrote that these angels who sinned were sent to 'hell', and put into gloomy dungeons to be held for judgment. There are three words which are generally translated 'hell' in the *KJV*. The two common ones are *hades* and *gehenna*. However, the word here is neither of those. In fact it is quite unique. It is *tartaroo* and in the Bible occurs only here, and for more on this word and the subject of angels being kept for judgment, please see Appendices 1 and 2.

We need to remember that Peter was writing to the Jewish Christians of the dispersion. Many lived good and righteous lives but were surrounded by pagan immorality and lawlessness. Some may have been tempted and fell, others were greatly distressed by such a life-style. How could God let this go on? Peter's point in this section was that God was well aware of it. He would reward them for their righteous lifestyle but the wicked ... they would suffer, either in this life from natural consequences of their misbehaviour or from the miracles of judgment that occurred during the Acts period, or they would suffer on that final day of judgment. They could not escape.

2 Peter 2:10-11: **This is especially true of those who follow the corrupt desire of the sinful nature and despise authority. Bold and arrogant, these men are not afraid to slander celestial beings; yet even angels, although they are stronger and more powerful, do not bring slanderous accusations against such beings in the presence of the Lord.**

Acts of judgment, either in this life or later on the Day of Judgment, were going to fall specifically upon those who were corrupted by following the desires of their sinful nature. This desire to do their own thing resulted in them despising authority, and these appear to be religious men, of one religion or another, for they even slandered celestial beings. What precisely they were saying and who they were saying it about we may never know. However, Peter pointed out that not even angels, far more powerful than human beings, brought such accusation against such beings in the presence of the Lord. And Jude, dealing with the same issue, wrote:

> In the very same way, these dreamers pollute their own bodies, reject authority and slander celestial beings. But even the archangel Michael, when he was disputing with the devil about the body of Moses, did not dare to bring a slanderous accusation against him, but said, "The Lord rebuke you!" Yet these men speak abusively against whatever they do not understand; and what things they do understand by instinct, like unreasoning animals - these are the very things that destroy them. (Jude 8-10)

As said above, we may not know precisely what was said about whom. However, today I have heard quite a few Christians vehemently say this, that or the other about Satan ... yet the Archangel Michael simply said "The Lord rebuke you!"

2 Peter 2:12-14: **But these men blaspheme in matters they do not understand. They are like brute beasts, creatures of instinct, born only to be caught and destroyed, and like beasts they too will perish. They will be paid back with harm for the harm they have done. Their idea of pleasure is to carouse in broad daylight. They are blots and blemishes, revelling in**

their pleasures while they feast with you. With eyes full of adultery, they never stop sinning; they seduce the unstable; they are experts in greed - an accursed brood!

This is quite a tirade from Peter. These people indulge in any sin, in any place, at any time and as such are just like animals, but they will come to harm. Paul wrote something similar:

> Do not be deceived: God cannot be mocked. A man reaps what he sows. The one who sows to please his sinful nature, from that nature will reap destruction; the one who sows to please the Spirit, from the Spirit will reap eternal life. (Galatians 6:7-8)

The harm suffered by such a person may be in this life, either from natural causes or, at that time, by a judgment from God, or it may be on the day of judgement.

These people are also hypocrites, as the *Living Bible* makes clear.

> For they live in evil pleasure day after day. They are a disgrace and a stain among you, deceiving you by living in foul sin on the side while they join your love feasts as though they were honest men. (2 Peter 2:13)

Jude states similar things in his letter. He wrote, "These men are blemishes at your love feasts, eating with you without the slightest qualm - shepherds who feed only themselves," (verse 12). Thus these people were infiltrating the Christian groups, eating their food and preying particularly upon unstable and vulnerable women. They wanted only what they could get and in all things, not just food, they were greedy.

2 Peter 2:15-16: **They have left the straight way and wandered off to follow the way of Balaam son of Beor, who loved the wages of wickedness. But he was rebuked for his wrongdoing by a donkey - a beast without speech - who spoke with a man's voice and restrained the prophet's madness.**

Here Peter is referring to an incident recorded in Numbers chapters 22 to 24, and is likening these people to Balaam, who enjoyed the wages of wickedness – similar to those mentioned above, who circumcised Gentiles for 'dishonest' gain (Titus 1:10-11). Jude also refers to Balaam in verse 11 of his letter.

2 Peter 2:17-19: **These men are springs without water and mists driven by a storm. Blackest darkness is reserved for them. For they mouth empty, boastful words and, by appealing to the lustful desires of sinful human nature, they entice people who are just escaping from those who live in error. They promise them freedom, while they themselves are slaves of depravity - for a man is a slave to whatever has mastered him.**

Peter says these men are "springs without water" and they are as substantial as "mist". Jude says of them:

> They are clouds without rain, blown along by the wind;
> > autumn trees, without fruit and uprooted - twice dead.
> They are wild waves of the sea, foaming up their shame;
> > wandering stars, for whom blackest darkness has been reserved forever. (Jude 12-13)

These people were appealing to the lustful desires of human nature and they were preying upon and enticing those who had recently been converted to Christianity, people who were just escaping from the sins of a pagan life-style. They promised freedom, but they were leading people into slavery.

We hear similar things today. People should be free to decide for themselves whether they want to take certain drugs, to watch pornography, to drink excessively. Yet many become addicted. They become slaves to the alcohol, the drugs or the sex, and then, themselves become advocates for that life-style. And the pushers target the young, who know no better, and the vulnerable, who are so weak.

2 Peter 2:20-22: If they have escaped the corruption of the world by knowing our Lord and Saviour Jesus Christ and are again entangled in it and overcome, they are worse off at the end than they were at the beginning. It would have been better for them not to have known the way of righteousness, than to have known it and then to turn their backs on the sacred command that was passed on to them. Of them the proverbs are true: "A dog returns to its vomit," and, "A sow that is washed goes back to her wallowing in the mud."

To understand these verses we need to take them in their context, to follow Peter's line of argument. He was talking about false prophets who were exploiting the true believers, seducing them with fine words and enticing them into desires of the sinful nature.

Peter then embarks upon a *hypothetical* argument, indicated by his use of 'if'. 'If' these people had become believers in the Lord Jesus Christ and so had escaped the corruption of the world ... 'if' they then became entangled again with the ways of the world and were overcome with them ... 'if' that were the situation, they would be worse than they were before. He is not saying they *were* believers. He is making a comparison.

Christ also made similar statements and comparisons. Consider, for instance, these two passages and notice the use of the word 'if'.

> "*If* anyone will not welcome you or listen to your words, shake the dust off your feet when you leave that home or town. I tell you the truth, it will be more bearable for Sodom and Gomorrah on the day of judgment than for that town." (Matthew 10:14-15)

> "Woe to you, Korazin! Woe to you, Bethsaida! *If* the miracles that were performed in you had been performed in Tyre and Sidon, they would have repented long ago in sackcloth and ashes. But I tell you, it will be more bearable for Tyre and Sidon on the day of judgment than for you. And you, Capernaum, will you be lifted up to the skies? No, you will go down to the depths. *If* the miracles that were performed in you had been performed in Sodom, it would have remained to this day. But I tell you that it will be more bearable for Sodom on the day of judgment than for you." (Matthew 11:21-24)

Thus Peter, with such forceful statements, was trying to persuade his readers not to follow these false prophets and be seduced by their fine words. He did not want them to turn from the way of righteousness and become like dogs who return to their vomit (see Proverbs 26:11).

2 Peter

Chapter 3

2 Peter Chapter 3

2 Peter 3:1-2: **Dear friends, this is now my second letter to you. I have written both of them as reminders to stimulate you to whole-some thinking. I want you to recall the words spoken in the past by the holy prophets and the command given by our Lord and Saviour through your apostles.**

In this opening verse Peter clearly states the purpose for both of his letters. By reminding them of what they had been taught, he wanted to stimulate them into right thinking which would result in a righteous life style.

He also wanted them to recall what past prophets had said, and the commands of Christ given through the apostles. Peter had to deal with a difficult issue. As mentioned in the *Introduction*, at this time (i.e. during the time covered by the Acts of the Apostles) they taught that Christ was soon to return. If Israel repented then Christ would come back, as Acts 3:19-21 makes clear.

> Repent, then, and turn to God, so that your sins may be wiped out, that times of refreshing may come from the Lord, and that he may send the Messiah, who has been appointed for you – even Jesus. Heaven must receive him until the time comes for God to restore everything, as he promised long ago through his holy prophets.

If Israel repented He would return to the Mount of Olives as their King, setting up His righteous kingdom upon this earth, the focus of the disciples' question in Acts 1:6. Now these groups of Jews to whom Peter wrote were Christians, they had repented and were anticipating His return so ... where was Christ? Living in small communities they were probably unaware of the bigger picture. Certainly many of the 'ordinary' Jews believed but not the leadership, neither people in influential positions (like synagogue rulers), nor the wealthy.

2 Peter 3:3-4: **First of all, you must understand that in the last days scoffers will come, scoffing and following their own evil desires. They will say, "Where is this 'coming' he promised? Ever since our fathers died, everything goes on as it has since the beginning of creation."**

First, from this statement, we can see that Peter considers the time in which he was living 'the last days'; the days leading up to Christ's return. At that time they should expect these false prophets who would scoff at the truth. This is not dissimilar to what happened in Jeremiah's day (see the comments on 2 Peter 2:1). Jeremiah gave a prophecy from the Lord saying that Babylon would come to conquer Jerusalem and all who surrendered and went out of the city would be spared. The false prophets said 'No!' The Babylonians would not conquer the city and people should stay in Jerusalem and fight.

Here Peter was still encouraging the Jews to repent and turn to Christ, teaching that He would then return. 'No!' said these false prophets, these scoffers. They claimed that such a thing would *never* happen. God will *never* intervene because, they said, He never has because "everything goes on as it has since the beginning of creation".

Remember that at the time Peter wrote, the opposition to the Christian Jews came from other Jews who refused to accept that Jesus was the Christ (Messiah) and Son of God. They were the religious leaders. Thus Peter says of them that they 'deliberately' forget ...

2 Peter 3:5-6: **But they deliberately forget that long ago by God's word the heavens existed and the earth was formed out of water and by water. By these waters also the world of that time was deluged and destroyed.**

Peter again goes back to Genesis to show that their argument was wrong. God did intervene; He did act on this earth. These false prophets, these religious leaders, knew this, but they deliberately turned a blind eye to it.

In those days leading up to the flood God was slow to act and judge, and Peter alludes to this a little later.

2 Peter 3:7-9: **By the same word the present heavens and earth are reserved for fire, being kept for the day of judgment and destruction of ungodly men. But do not forget this one thing, dear friends: With the Lord a day is like a thousand years, and a thousand years are like a day. The Lord is not slow in keeping his promise, as some understand slowness. He is patient with you, not wanting anyone to perish, but everyone to come to repentance.**

In Genesis God made a covenant with Noah, stating that He would never again destroy the earth by flood (Genesis 9:9-13). Having just mentioned this flood, Peter then wrote that the next time the world, and in fact both the present heavens and earth, are to be destroyed it is to be with fire. This event will take place at the Day of Judgment when all the ungodly are destroyed. John seems to be talking of this towards the end of Revelation. There we read of judgment and the creation of a new heavens and new earth.

> Then I saw a great white throne and him who was seated on it. Earth and sky fled from his presence, and there was no place for them. And I saw the dead, great and small, standing before the throne, and books were opened. Another book was opened, which is the book of life. The dead were judged according to what they had done as recorded in the books. The sea gave up the dead that were in it, and death and Hades gave up the dead that were in them, and each person was judged according to what he had done. Then death and Hades were thrown into the lake of fire. The lake of fire is the second death. If anyone's name was not found written in the book of life, he was thrown into the lake of fire. (Revelation 20:11-15)

> Then I saw a new heaven and a new earth, for the first heaven and the first earth had passed away, and there was no longer any sea. I saw the Holy City, the new Jerusalem, coming down out of heaven from God, prepared as a bride beautifully dressed for her husband. And I heard a loud voice from the throne saying, "Now the dwelling of God is with men, and he will live with them. They will be his people, and God himself will be with them and be their God. He will wipe every tear from their eyes. There will be no more death or mourning or crying or pain, for the old order of things has passed away." He who was seated on the throne said, "I am making everything new!" Then he said, "Write this down, for these words are trustworthy and true." (Revelation 21:1-5)

Having reminded them of this future judgment and destruction, Peter returned to the theme of God's patience. God was slow in sending the Genesis flood. The name 'Methuselah' means 'when he is dead it shall be sent'; i.e. the flood. And Methuselah was the longest living human being, a demonstration of God's longsuffering and patience, giving mankind the opportunity to repent and change their ways, but they did not and corruption and violence filled the earth (Genesis 6:11) .

Similarly, in Peter's day, God was not slow to keep His promise of sending Christ back. He wanted to give everyone the opportunity to repent. When the nation of Israel repented, then He would send back the Christ (Acts 3:19-21). He was waiting on them.

2 Peter 3:10-12: **But the day of the Lord will come like a thief. The heavens will disappear with a roar; the elements will be destroyed by fire, and the earth and everything in it will be laid bare. Since everything will be destroyed in this way, what kind of people ought you to be? You ought to live holy and godly lives as you look forward to the day of God and speed its coming. That day will bring about the destruction of the heavens by fire, and the elements will melt in the heat.**

There are certain expressions which can mislead us if we do not understand them. For example, some believe that the expression 'The Last Days' *always* refers to the days leading up to the second coming of Christ. However, a careful study of this expression throughout the Bible shows this *not* to be the case[5],

---

[5] See *The Last Days! When?* by Michael Penny, published by the Open Bible Trust. In this every occurrence of 'The Last Days' and related expressions is considered and placed in its context. Also available as an eBook

and the *NIV* often translates it 'in days to come', allowing the context to determine the time.

The same is true of 'The Day of the Lord'[6]. Some people state that this *always* refers to the time leading up to Christ's return; the great and terrible Day of the Lord when Israel shall suffer from the great tribulation (Matthew 24:21-29). Quite often, when this expression occurs, there is some form of distress and destruction. However, Peter's usage of 'the day of God' here has nothing to do with the return of Christ. Rather, he uses the expression to refer to the day when the heavens and earth disappear and are destroyed.

If this is to be the end of this world then, he states, they should live holy and good lives, but what does he mean by them being able to 'speed its coming'? This again refers to what Peter said in Acts 3:19-21; if Israel repented, then Christ would return and after His thousand year reign on earth, then the judgment and destruction would come (Revelation 20). However, if they did not repent, then Christ would not return at that time. We know from the New Testament documents, and especially the Acts of the Apostles, that they did not repent. At the end of Acts the nation had so hardened their hearts that they rendered themselves blind to the miracles and deaf to the arguments. Thus God's salvation was sent to the Gentiles (Acts 28:25-28). God has followed this new course of action for nearly 2,000 years so the events Peter wrote about were slowed down, rather than speeded up. However, one day the nation of Israel will again become centre stage in

---

[6] See *The Day of the Lord! When?* by Michael Penny, published by the Open Bible Trust. In this every occurrence of 'The Day of the Lord' and related expressions is considered and placed in its context. Available as an eBook.

God's plan and the unfulfilled prophecies relating to them will be accomplished.

2 Peter 3:13-14: But in keeping with his promise we are looking forward to a new heaven and a new earth, the home of righteousness. So then, dear friends, since you are looking forward to this, make every effort to be found spotless, blameless and at peace with him.

Peter then mentioned the new heavens and new earth. In this new creation John states that "There will be no more death or mourning or crying or pain, for the old order of things has passed away" (Revelation 21:4). Thus there is no more sin and Peter says this new creation is "the home of righteousness". The inherent characteristic of the current creation is 'sin' (Romans 3:10,23). However, that of the new creation will be 'righteousness', and believers are told that they, too, will be righteous in resurrection (2 Corinthians 5:21). If that be the case, wrote Peter, they should make every effort, here and now, to live spotless and blameless lives, and be at peace with God.

2 Peter 3:15-16: Bear in mind that our Lord's patience means salvation, just as our dear brother Paul also wrote to you with the wisdom that God gave him. He writes the same way in all his letters, speaking in them of these matters. His letters contain some things that are hard to understand, which ignorant and unstable people distort, as they do the other Scriptures, to their own destruction.

Peter again reminded his readers of God's patience, but then goes on to mention the writings of Paul. It has been a puzzle to many as to which letters Peter is referring. Peter wrote to the dispersed Jews in Pontus, Galatia, Cappadocia, Asia and Bithynia.

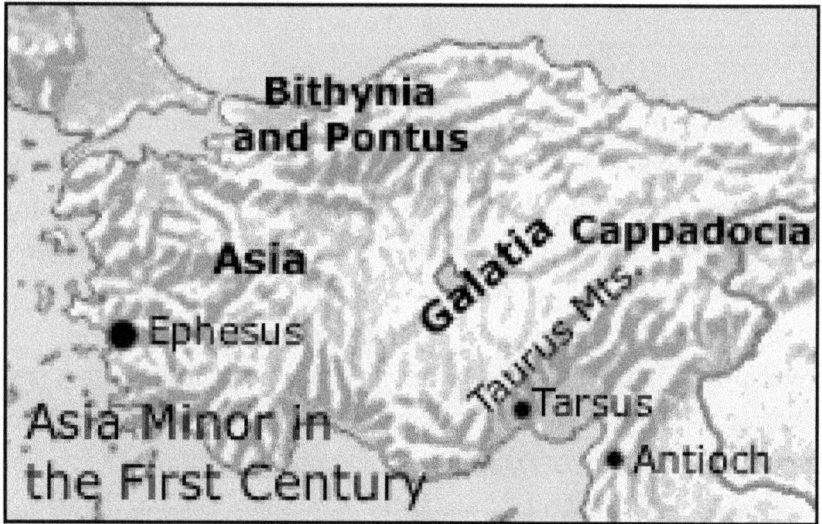

Asia Minor in the First Century

During the Acts Period Paul wrote to the Galatians, Thessalonians, Corinthians and Romans, and Peter wrote this second letter towards the end of the Acts period. In that case Paul may have written all six of those letters by this time. However, consultation with a map shows that none of Thessalonica, Corinth and Rome lay in the regions to which Peter was writing. Only the letter to the Galatians, Paul's first, fits the bill. However, some consider that Paul wrote Hebrews. If that were the case, there would be no problem, as the letter to the Hebrews deals with some of the issues which Peter wrote about.

But what was it in Paul's letters that people found hard to understand, and which they distorted? Note that Peter stated that not only did they distort what Paul wrote, they also distorted the other 'Scriptures'. Two points arise from this; the people distorting both Paul and the other Scriptures would have been Jews, as the Gentile at that time did not consider what we call the Old Testament to be inspired 'Scripture'. Second, from the statement 'as they do the *other* Scriptures' means that Peter considered Paul's writings to be 'Scripture', on a par with the Old Testament.

So what was it that those Jews found hard to understand in Paul's letters? Two obvious things were the Gentiles being grafted into the olive tree of Israel (Romans 11:13-18), and the fact that these Gentile converts to Christians did not have to be circumcised (Acts 15:1-2,5). That issue prompted the Jerusalem Council of Acts 15 and was the reason Paul wrote the letter to the Galatians.

We know that Peter, himself, had difficulty accepting the former (see Galatians 2:11-14). As for the latter, even though the council of Jerusalem decreed that Gentiles did not have to be circumcised, some Christian Jews continued to insist that they must (Titus 1:10-11).

Also, in the earlier letters of Paul, as mentioned in the *Introduction*, Paul also referred to the nearness of Christ's return, and the problems which would arise in the days preceding it. Certainly his teaching was distorted in Thessalonica; someone even wrote a letter, saying it was from Paul, but the teaching in that bogus letter distorted what Paul had been teaching (2 Thessalonians 2:2).

2 Peter 3:17-18: **Therefore, dear friends, since you already know this, be on your guard so that you may not be carried away by the error of lawless men and fall from your secure position. But grow in the grace and knowledge of our Lord and Saviour Jesus Christ. To him be glory both now and forever! Amen.**

And so Peter concludes the letter by warning them to be on their guard against these false teachers, these lawless men. He did not want them to fall from their secure position. This is not referring to their salvation as that is by grace and is guaranteed (Romans 4:16). However, it is their reward, their prize which they can lose.

> For no one can lay any foundation other than the one already laid, which is Jesus Christ. If any man builds on this foundation using gold, silver, costly stones, wood, hay or straw, his work will be shown for what it is, because the Day will bring it to light. It will be revealed with fire, and the fire will test the quality of each man's work. If what he has built survives, he will receive his reward. If it is burned up, he will suffer loss; he himself will be saved, but only as one escaping through the flames. (1 Corinthians 3:11-15)

> Do not let anyone who delights in false humility and the worship of angels disqualify you for the prize. Such a person goes into great detail about what he has seen, and his unspiritual mind puffs him up with idle notions. (Colossians 2:18)

> Not that I have already obtained all this, or have already been made perfect, but I press on to take hold of that for which Christ Jesus took hold of me. Brothers, I do not consider myself yet to have taken hold of it. But one thing I do: Forgetting what is behind and straining toward what is ahead, I press on toward the goal to win the prize for which God has called me heavenwards in Christ Jesus. (Philippians 3:12-14)

Peter did not want his readers to be tempted to backslide and fall away. Rather he wanted them to grow in grace and grow in the knowledge of Jesus, the Son of God, their Messiah (Christ) and Saviour.

Those words are equally applicable to us living in the 21st century. The temptations and trials may be different, but we have desires which belong to our sinful nature and there are elements in our society which continually tempt and test us in such areas. We must resist and overcome and grow in grace and love, gaining a greater knowledge of our Lord Jesus Christ and a better understanding of just what God's plan is for the age in which we live. Our aim should be to lives which will bring Him glory, honour and praise.

Appendix 1:

Tartarus

Appendix 1:
Tartarus

The word translated 'hell' in 2 Peter 2:4 is *tartaroo* and occurs only here in the Bible. It is also very rare in early religious literature. It does occur in *The Book of Enoch*.

> And these are the names of the holy angels who watch. Uriel, one of the holy angels, who is over the world and over Tartarus. (Chapter 20, 1-2)

The Book of Enoch was written during the second century BC and is an example of apocryphal Jewish writing. This book is also referred to by Jude (see verse 14) who also quotes from another apocryphal book, *The Assumption of Moses* (see verse 9-10).

The Hellenized Jew Philo of Alexandria (20 BC to 50 AD) also referred to *tartarus* in his writings, and Walter Bauer, in his *A Greek-English Lexicon of the New Testament and Other Early Christian Literature*, says the following:

> Tartarus, thought by the Greeks as a subterranean place lower than Hades where divine punishments were meted out, was so regarded in Jewish apocalyptic as well.

Appendix 2:

Angels in dungeons for judgment

Appendix 2:
Angels in dungeons
for judgment

God did not spare angels when they sinned, but sent them to hell, putting them into gloomy dungeons to be held for judgment. (2 Peter 2:4)

There seems to be three types of beings, or three states:
1. immortal
2. mortal
3. a-mortal.

Immortal

In fact, the Bible tells us that there is only one being who is immortal.

> God, the blessed and only Ruler, the King of kings and Lord of lords, who alone is immortal. (1 Timothy 6:15-16)

> Now to the King eternal, immortal, invisible, the only God, be honour and glory for ever and ever. Amen. (1 Timothy 1:17)

This comes as somewhat of a surprise to many people but God alone is the only one who is immortal. This means that neither angels, nor humans, are immortal; neither Satan, nor the Archangel Michael.

Mortal

Human beings are not immortal; there is nothing about us that is immortal. However, we do have the potential to become immortal.

> Listen, I tell you a mystery: We will not all sleep, but we will all be changed - in a flash, in the twinkling of an eye, at the last trumpet. For the trumpet will sound, the dead will be raised imperishable, and we will be changed. For the perishable must clothe itself with the imperishable, and the mortal with immortality. When the perishable has been clothed with the imperishable, and the mortal with immortality, then the saying that is written will come true: "Death has been swallowed up in victory." (1 Corinthians 15:51-54)

Those who believe in the Christ will be given immortality on the day He returns, either through resurrection or, for those who are alive, through being changed[7].

A-mortal

It would appear that the angels, and beings such as the Archangel Michael and Satan, are a-mortal. This means that they do not die, as mortal beings do, but can be destroyed or can live for ever. It would seem that the devil and his angels are to be destroyed but that Michael and the other angels will live for ever.

---

[7] For more on these subjects see *Resurrection! When?* by Sylvia and Michael Penny and *Immortality! When?* by Michael Penny. Both published by The Open Bible Trust.

Some may be surprised at the idea of Satan being destroyed but we read of this in Hebrews 2:14, referring to Christ we read, "by his death he might destroy him who holds the power of death - that is, the devil." The word 'destroy' here is the Greek *katergeo* which, according to Arndt & Gingrich, means to "make ineffective, powerless, idle". How is this to be achieved? The answer may lie in Ezekiel 28:12-19, a passage which refers to Satan. There we read:

> So I made a fire come out from you, and it consumed you, and I reduced you to ashes on the ground in the sight of all who were watching. All the nations who knew you are appalled at you; you have come to a horrible end and will be no more. (Ezekiel 28:18-19)

Thus Satan is destroyed by fire and in Matthew 25:41 the Lord speaks of "the eternal fire prepared for the devil and his angels" and it is this fire of judgment that Peter may have been referring to in 2 Peter 2:4.

However, some may protest and quote Revelation 20:10:

> And the devil, who deceived them, was thrown into the lake of burning sulphur, where the beast and the false prophet had been thrown. They will be tormented day and night for ever and ever.

Some claim this refers to eternal punishment, rather than destruction. However, the expression translated "for ever and ever" means, literally, "to the age of the ages". First note that it is 'to' a point in time and shows that this is not an eternal punishment. It is up to a point in time.

We understand expressions like 'King of kings' and 'Lord of lord'; the supreme king, the highest lord. Thus the 'age of the ages' is the supreme age which, from the information we have in the Bible, is the creation of the new heavens and new earth, the home of righteousness. In this new creation there "will be no more death or mourning or crying or pain, for the old order of things has passed away" (Revelation 21:4). Thus there is no pain or torment, the former things, including Satan and his angels and torment, will have passed away. They will have received their judgment.

Also in this Series

Michael Penny has written a number of other books in this series including:

Studies in Ruth

Studies in 1 Thessalonians

Studies in 2 Thessalonians

Studies in Colossians

Studies in Philemon

Studies in 1 Timothy

Studies in 2 Timothy

Studies in Titus

Studies in John's Epistles

Studies in Jude

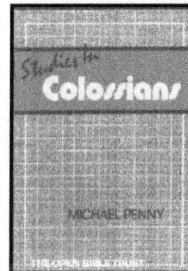

These publications, and many more, are available from the Open Bible. For a full list please visit

www.obt.org.uk

About the author

Michael Penny was born in Ebbw Vale, Gwent, Wales in 1943. He read Mathematics at the University of Reading, before teaching for twelve years and becoming the Director of Mathematics and Business Studies at Queen Mary's College Basingstoke in Hampshire, England. In 1978 he entered Christian publishing, and in 1984 became the administrator of The Open Bible Trust.

He held this position for seven years, before moving to the USA and becoming pastor of Grace Church in New Berlin, Wisconsin. He returned to Britain in 1999, and is at present the Administrator and Editor of The Open Bible Trust. From 2010 he has been Chairman of Churches Together in Reading, where he speaks in a number of churches of different denominations. He is also a member of the Advisory Committee to Reading University Christian Union and a chaplain at Reading College.

He is lead chaplain for Activate Learning and has set up chaplaincy teams in a number of their colleges including Reading College, The City of Oxford College, Bracknell and Wokingham College, and Blackbird Leys College.

He lives near Reading with his wife and has appeared on Premier Radio and BBC Radio Berkshire many times. He has made several speaking tours of America, Canada, Australia, New Zealand and the Netherlands, as well as others to South Africa and the Philippines. Some of his writings have been translated into German and Russian.

Studies in 2 Peter

Also by Michael Penny

He has written many books including:

40 Problem Passages,
Galatians: Interpretation and Application,
Joel's Prophecy: Past and Future,
Approaching the Bible,
The Miracles of the Apostles,
The Manual on the Gospel of John
The Bible! Myth or Message?

Plus two written with W M Henry:

The Will of God: Past and Present
Following Philippians.

His latest three books are:

James: His life and letter
Peter: His life and letters.
Paul: A Missionary of Genius

Further details of all these books can be seen on

www.obt.org.uk

from where they can also be ordered.

They are also available as eBooks from Amazon and Apple and
as KDP paperbacks from Amazon.

Further details of the books on these pages
can be seen on

www.obt.org.uk

The books are available from that website and from

The Open Bible Trust
Fordland Mount, Upper Basildon,
Reading, RG8 8LU, UK.

They are also available as eBooks from Amazon and
Apple and as
KDP paperback from Amazon

Further Reading

Salvation

Safe and Secure

Sylvia Penny

This important book is a thorough treatment of the subject of salvation, asking such questions as ...

- **What is it, exactly, that saves us?**
- **Is salvation secure?**
- **Can it be lost?**
- **What is 'conditional security'?**

It deals with a wide number of issues such as ...

Salvation and works	**The doctrine of rewards**
Lordship salvation	**Free grace theology**
Assurance of salvation	**Why people lose their faith**

Further details of all these books can be seen on **www.obt.org.uk** from where they can also be ordered.

They are also available as eBooks from Amazon and Apple and as KDP paperbacks from Amazon.

About this book

Studies in 2 Peter

The introduction deals with three important questions:

- · To whom did Peter write?
- · When did he write?
- · Why did he write?

The answers to these set the tone for the exposition of this short letter, much of which is clear teaching and encouragement. However, there are some difficult passages.

These include Peter's use of the word 'tartarus' and his statement about 'angels held in dungeons for judgment'. Additional clarifying comments on these are given in an appendix.

Publications of The Open Bible Trust must be in accordance with its evangelical, fundamental and dispensational basis. However, beyond this minimum, writers are free to express whatever beliefs they may have as their own understanding, provided that the aim in so doing is to further the object of The Open Bible Trust. A copy of the doctrinal basis is available on **www.obt.org.uk** or from:

THE OPEN BIBLE TRUST
Fordland Mount, Upper Basildon,
Reading, RG8 8LU, UK.